Out of the Corner of Your Eye

Published by Mission Point Press
2554 Chandler Rd.
Traverse City, MI 49696
(231) 421-9513
MissionPointPress.com

ISBN: 978-1-954786-51-6

Printed in the United States of America

OUT OF THE CORNER OF YOUR EYE

Seeing the Things that Matter

Richard Fidler

MISSION POINT PRESS

CONTENTS

Introduction

How wonderful the world is! What happens every moment in the sky, on earth, and in the water is enough to astound both angels and infidels. This book is written in appreciation of it all—waves in sand and water, trees sculpted by the wind, the rise and fall of hills, the play of shadows under the canopies of trees, the unlikely appearance of life in unlikely places, the glorious appearance of rainbows and halos in the sky. All these phenomena are there for us to see, yet we pay no attention to them, save for those years of childhood when we had not learned to tune them out. I would have us return to that time when shadows and patterns of light entranced us, when insects engaged us, when the sounds of nature ever surprised and puzzled us. That is the purpose of this book—to wake us up.

This is not a science textbook, though at times it offers glimpses into research on certain topics. Rather, it is a book about exploring the natural world and asking questions about it. With utmost respect for science—I was a science teacher for 31 years—I offer a different perspective on the world than most practicing scientists: I freely use the word *love* when I talk about nature. Often that love for the evolved universe is expressed by means of poems and haiku written by authors with like feelings for the world. Poems are better than prose at telling the mood of the heart.

A video screen is a poor substitute for the real world. Images found there bear the mark of human creation, in the selection of the stories told and in the perspective offered to the viewer. Often the object is to sell something: a product, a religious or political point of view, or a contrived montage designed to change behavior in ways deemed salutary for society. By contrast, nature does not sell anything, nor is its perspective human-centered. It takes no sides—predator vs. prey, humans vs. viruses, life vs. non-life.

In three bold words the *Tao Te Ching* says, "Tien bu jen." Heaven (nature) is not "jen," that character written in two parts, "man" and the numeral "two." The meaning is clear. Nature has nothing to do with social doings of men. That insight is both terrifying and illuminating: terrifying because when things go bad, we want to believe everything will turn out all right, and illuminating because we are embedded in a vast web of nature, participating as all living and non-living things do, each in its own way. Viewed that way, our deaths are hardly to be feared.

In the broadest sense, all living things interact with each other either directly or indirectly. A right whale is influenced by a pink lady's slipper, however numberless the links of causation. That said, this book is anchored in a specific place at a specific time: the Traverse City area in the year 2021. Traverse City is a moderate-sized city isolated from larger population centers and located about a hundred miles south (160 km) of the Straits of Mackinac. Many natural communities lie nearby: the Sleeping Bear Lakeshore, pine barrens, temperate hardwood forests, boreal swamps, bogs, and many others. Before white settlement great stands of white and yellow (red) pine grew on the sandy soils left by the glacier only a few thousands of years previous. They were cut down in a frenzy of activity—never to return in their former size or abundance—to build structures in Chicago, Detroit, or other great cities of the time. Currently, commercial, industrial, and residential development are changing the landscape nearly as much as the loggers of the past did. Change never ceases.

This is the location in time and space that gives rise to this book. Though it speaks of Northern Michigan, its stories touch all Americans—indeed, all people. After all, the majesty of the sky is just as available to an African as to a resident of Grand Traverse county. Shadows intrigue children in China as they do in America. Waves spread on lakes in Europe as well as in Michigan. Waking up to the vibrant life of nature can occur anywhere. Out of the corner of our eyes, let us see the things that matter.

Finally, I wish to thank Mission Point Press and Heather Shaw for making this book beautiful and readable. What a joy it has been working with them!

Richard Fidler, October, 2021

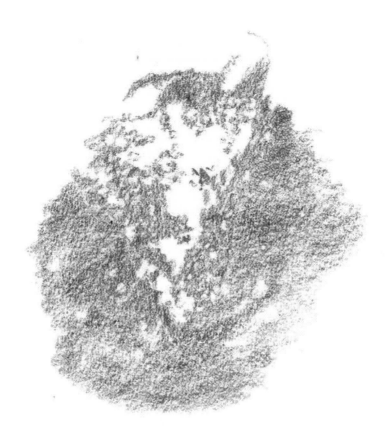

The velvety fingers of shadows

As we grow out of toddlerhood, we forget about shadows. My daughter paid attention to patterns of light and dark when she was three, pointing to a rare spot of sunlight on the floor in February and inquiring earnestly, "What dat?" We tune shadows out even as they occupy large blocks of our visual field, so concentrated we are on the things that seem to matter, the objects that cast the shadows. But we have cast shadows aside too quickly. Let us re-create that inquiring mind of my daughter when we ask about shadows, "What dat?"

The shadow of an object held close to a surface appears sharply defined and dark in outline, becoming blurry at the edges as we move it away at increasing distances. The darkest part of the shadow is the umbra: a sensor within it would detect no part of the light source. The blurry part is the penumbra, the region of the shadow that allows some light from the source to penetrate. Big things and small things alike cast shadows. As the moon enters the Earth's shadow during a lunar eclipse, it first encounters the penumbra, then later at totality, the umbra.

A dappled walkway under a shade tree is a quilt of shadows and bright spots, and in some respects, it is exactly that. But some of the patches of light we see are not due to the sun penetrating the canopy of the tree, but are images of the sun projected by rays gathering at tiny holes in the leaves, then spreading out on a surface to make visible the whole solar disk. These pinhole projections produce round images of the sun near midday and elliptical ones near sunrise and sunset. A partial eclipse reveals multiple images of the indented sun cast over hoods of cars, sidewalks, and other smooth surfaces. The effect is enchanting.

What color are shadows? We want to think they are black, but are they? Under some circumstances, they not even dark. On a walk I pass under a chain-link mesh designed to keep things from dropping onto pedestrians. When I hold a white canvas bag under it on a sunny day, as expected it shows dark lines for the wires and bright squares in between. But as I move it lower, the shadow becomes blurred, and at about seven feet from the mesh, it flips with bright lines and dark squares. Still lower, the shadows disappear altogether.

I am informed the phenomenon is called shadow inversion, but am unsure what causes it.

Cast shadows can have different colors. In winter I once observed blue shadows cast on the white snow of a parking lot by orange sodium-vapor overhead lights. Both the color of the light source and the surface upon which the shadow is cast affect the way shadows appear. Would the orange and red colors of a setting sun make shadows look blue or purple? I suspect so.

Shadows, by themselves, are commonly ignored because "real objects" interact with us directly. Still, shadows give us much pleasure as they give us respite from the summer sun and provide hiding places for things we love. In her diary six-year-old Opal Whitely speaks of the tenderness and peace shadows can bring. She introduces a blind girl (who might be able to see patches of light and dark) to shadows:

> *Today near even-time I did lead*
> *the girl who has no seeing*
> *a little way into the forest*
> *where it was darkness and shadows were.*
> *I led her towards a shadow*
> *that was coming our way.*
> *It did touch her cheeks*
> *with its velvety fingers.*
> *And now she too*
> *Does have likings for shadows.*
> *And her fear that was is gone.*
> Opal: *The Journal of an Understanding Heart*

OUT OF THE CORNER OF YOUR EYE

Like Opal, I love shadows. Here is my take on them:

Crisp the shadows of grass stalks on pavement
Blotched are those of tree leaves above.
Dancing patches on the walk, sketches of the sun:
Look up at the leafy canopy and see them for yourself—
The sun's disk comes and goes with the wind.
Behind a thin veil of cirrus,
Does the muted light still cast shadows?
Yes!—adumbrated upon light smooth surfaces only.
They lurk—no, play—in the recesses of our minds
Occupying spaces there long forgotten
Things for babies to wonder at
Before they enter the world of human things.
Shadows harbor fairies, goblins, and elves
Within the darkest shade.
We only see them when we walk
And peek out of the corners of our eyes.

Dandelions: Zen monks of spring

Love them or hate them—there is little ground in between when it comes to dandelions. They come early, brightening lawns and waste places with rich yellow blossoms in April and May, attracting bees and other pollinators with generous offerings of nectar and pollen, and delighting children with their feathery seeds. My gang used to recite, "Momma had a baby and its head popped off!" as they snapped off the flowering heads. Aside from that fun, they are said to be good to eat—though I have been unimpressed with their taste and texture. On the other hand, they are obnoxious interlopers to fastidious keepers of lawns, and are nearly impossible to get rid of without exertion to extract their endless taproots or else without the application of herbicides. The puffy heads of seeds that raise themselves above lesser plants are testimony to the lawnkeepers' neglect.

Let us look at dandelions in another way. How are they so wonderfully adapted to life on American suburban lawns? How did these invaders from Europe manage to conquer the North American continent so rapidly, overspreading it in only a few hundred years? Why will they persist as long as humans keep gardens and lawns in spite of all the measures we take to control them? Given their success in nature, do they have lessons to teach us about survival in inhospitable environments? I believe they do.

The form of the plant predisposes it to colonizing lawns. Its leaves are in a tight rosette that clings to the earth. Offering no tender shoots above the blades of grass nearby, it escapes the whirling blades of the lawn mower. Flower buds—several for each plant—lie low until warm weather triggers their rapid growth. In the space of two or three weeks they come to bloom all at once, sending pollinators into frenzy. If cold rainy weather inhibits bees and butterflies, flowers can self-pollinate or even begin to develop seeds without pollination at all, an unlikely adaptation in the plant world.

As seeds mature, the plant makes ready to launch them from elevated platforms. Flower stalks extend four, five, and six (10–15 cm) inches in the space of a few days if conditions are favorable. Meanwhile, silken hairs grow from a thread-like stalk attached to each seed, forming a miniature parachute. The spring breeze carries them away, some journeys lasting but a moment, but others, an hour, a

Homage to dandelion

week, or a month. That is the way this adventurous plant escapes the dangers of hoe and herbicides. It gets out when the getting is good.

Most of them will fail to find a good place to grow. They will land in a stream or lake and decompose under water in a few days, or else land on surfaces that will not yield to the tender root that comes out of the seed coat. Many others will be eaten by insects or birds. But one or two out of each hundred will find a suitable place to grow—perhaps a lawn like the one it came from, or perhaps the disturbed ground around a construction site. There it will push down its taproot and gather energy to weather the long winter, perhaps under a cover of snow and ice.

Dandelions have lived in North American since the Mayflower brought them over from Europe in 1620, if not before. Wherever settlers sowed their crops, the yellow heads appeared among the wheat and oats, the sight no doubt gladdening hearts to see a familiar sign of spring. The first floral assessment of Michigan records them in Kalamazoo in 1838. Wherever farmers went with their seeds, dandelions followed. It was a continent ripe for colonization, not just by white settlers but by the friendly yellow flowers they inadvertently brought with them.

Were they opportunists, taking advantage of wagon and plow to conquer the land? Yes, but isn't that judgment too harsh? Dandelions were supremely adapted to life close to human habitation, wherever the forest was leveled to make space for farms and cities. They made prodigious amounts of seed, developed means to distribute them widely, and laid low when lying low was advantageous for survival. They literally threw their fate to the winds, and reaped the benefits of that strategy.

Is that a lesson for us? To take chances to improve our lot? Most white settlers came to this land with exactly that goal in mind. They accepted the risk of failure to achieve success for themselves and their children to come. Unlike humans, dandelions do not display courage, but only a winning strategy for their continued existence on Earth, a strategy well-designed since they have plenty of offspring to subject to the grand experiment. In the end, does it matter that 99 seeds fail to become a mature plant? The one that achieves success

ensures the survival of the species. With something less than death facing us if we fail to accomplish a goal, is it not worthwhile to take a risk?

Dandelions are the Zen monks of the plant kingdom. In the China of 1200 years ago wandering monks would go out to search for wisdom with only a knapsack as their luggage. Walking mountain paths alone, eating wild foods they came across, occasionally stopping at monasteries to visit resident teachers, they were called *unsui*, a word made up of two characters, one denoting clouds and the other water. The expression is shortened from a longer line in a Chinese poem that translates "moving like clouds, flowing like water," an accurate description of monks and dandelion seeds. One seeks wisdom, the other a good place to grow. I respect them both.

Bending with the wind

On the foredune only a few feet from the shore a small white pine bends away from the crash of waves and the twenty mile-per-hour (32 kph) wind that drives them. Unlike its brothers and sisters in the forest, it is asymmetric, with most of its needles and branches pointed landward, away from the prevailing westerly wind. It hardly seems a member of the same species that colonized Northern Michigan after the ice departed, many of those trees growing to a height of two-thirds the length of a football field in dense stands that covered thousands of acres. Like a pitiful waif it

Wood thickens on opposite sides of bent stems

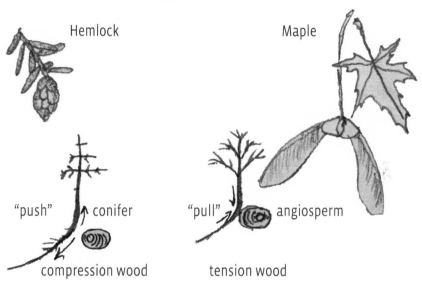

Hemlock

Maple

"push" ↑ conifer

compression wood

"pull" angiosperm

tension wood

struggles to maintain life in this harsh beach habitat. Its needles are tougher than its forest relatives, and shorter—about 1.5 inches (3.5 cm) long, as compared to the four-inch (10 cm) needles on white pines sheltered in the forest. Many of them are yellowing, fighting the desiccating effect of a hot summer wind on this June day. How does a tree like this adapt to the assault of bitter winds and drying heat? That is the question that engages me as I sketch its outline in my notebook.

As white pines are bent and twisted by the wind, they respond to the stress and to gravity in a prescribed way. If they are tipped to one side, they strengthen their stems by growing thick-walled xylem cells away from the bend, forming a brace on the outside. Trees with flowers do it the opposite way: the brace of xylem grows on the inside, pulling it upright. Either way, how does the tree "know" to make the braces—what is the signal that compels it to respond to the force of gravity? Preliminary studies of one plant species point to activation of hundreds of genes within 30 minutes of mechanical disruption—but where are the sensors located in the cell and how are they turned on? Why are some species more prone to respond to mechanical stress than others? Some questions do not have ready answers. Is it better for a wanderer to simply wonder rather than to seek out answers on the Internet? For me, it often is.

Germans have a name for trees that are wind-swept and bent away from drying winds: *krummholz*, (literally, "bent wood"). Mostly the term applies to stunted or deformed trees growing in arctic waste-lands that endure long days of howling winds. Growth in such trees is very dense, close to the ground with branches extending away from the prevailing winds. In milder climates they may take a one-sided appearance and are called flag or banner trees. That is how they look at the shores of the Great Lakes.

Japanese aesthetic prizes the asymmetry of flag trees. If prevailing winds will not shape them naturally, gardeners will bend branches with sturdy wires to provide the stress required to stimulate the growth of xylem on the outside of conifers. Appropriate trimming will complete the windswept look. For the Japanese, strong pre-vailing winds are not necessary to create the krummolz effect.

The wonder of it all is that plants are aware of mechanical stress and respond to it in predictable ways. We know they react to light with shoots bending towards the source, and we know they react to gravity with roots growing downward no matter the orientation of seeds or bulbs, but their reaction to the blowing wind is not something we often think about. The sensory world of plants is wider than we imagine.

Here is a poem I wrote about a white pine tree growing on a secluded beach on Grand Traverse Bay, Michigan.

Krummolz

Bent it is, and dwarfed,
the wind dries its yellowing needles,
pruning back the branches that offer resistance.
A few needles fall
on to an alyssum that grows below,
its two white flowers bent low,
nearly touching the sand.
A single pod stands ready
to shed its seeds
into the stinging wind above.

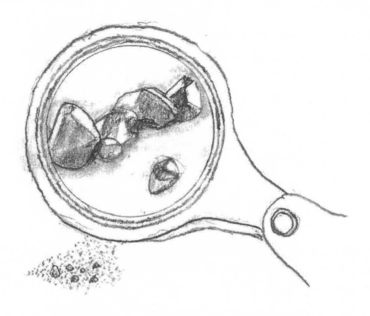

Singing sand: the voice of secluded beaches

To see a World in a Grain of Sand
And a Heaven in a Wild Flower
Hold Infinity in the palm of your hand
And Eternity in an hour
  —William Blake, *Auguries of Innocence*

I was startled the first time I heard sand squawk. With my geology class, I was on a secluded beach unspoiled by tourists and their pets. Our professor had us go to a place just up from where the waves came up at the shore, where the sand was dry at the surface, becoming moist only a few centimeters lower. At his direction, we moved our hands rapidly back and forth through the sand. Then came the sound—it sounded like a squawk to me, but some have called the sound "barking." When you scuff through it with your feet, it might sound like a barking dog, though not to my ears. The more common name—singing sand—did not seem to fit, either.

After the initial euphoria at the discovery died down, we carried samples of singing sand and ordinary sand back to the laboratory. How were they different? Sieving the sand, we found singing sand had a higher percentage of grains of the same size. They differed in brightness, too, with singing sand appearing less dirty—cleaner, in a sense. Individual grains took on a polish ordinary sand did not have. We found that singing sand could not be wet; it lost its voice under that condition.

What made the squawking sound? While answers are not crystal clear, it is believed that layers of clean, dry spherical grains slip past each other as the sand is compressed. At the same time, it might be nothing more than the way we kids used to chirp our athletic shoes on polished floors to the annoyance of adults around us—friction between objects making the sound. Either way, unpolished grains won't work because they would be slowed or impeded by imperfections. Wet sand won't sing either, as water holds the grains together. Whatever the exact cause, we know one thing for sure: pristine beaches are a must. Singing sands do not persist in the face of beach volleyball and other frolicking.

If sands sing, then what note do they favor? One study fixes the note at about A4 (450 Hz), but that is only on average since the thickness of the dry sand layer can affect the frequency of the sound. Deserts can produce the sound as well as beaches. Worldwide, the phenomenon is quite rare. Only 33 beach locations have been pinpointed as singing sand areas with Lake Michigan and Lake Superior beaches comprising two of them. Within Sleeping Bear Dunes National Lakeshore, I have found plenty of singing sand locations, especially on North Manitou and South Manitou islands, which are both protected from human traffic by their remoteness and by the watery moat of Lake Michigan.

The term "singing sand" has also been applied to something very different. Among sand dunes, occasionally slippages of sand—avalanches—can cause a rumble that can attain a loudness of more than 100 decibels, about the level of a motorcycle accelerating. Colorado's Great Sand Dunes National Park is known for such events, though it is not impossible that Sleeping Bear could experience the same thing.

Take time to visit a remote beach and scuff your feet in the dry sand above the packed sand moistened by the waves. You may be rewarded by the cheerful chirp of singing sands. Careful not to overdo it. You wouldn't want to scuff it so roughly that it stops singing!

it sings only if played
if played too much, it falls silent...
singing sand!

Living small in the city

Cities are challenging places for most organisms to live. With asphalt streets absorbing the sun's radiation, they must survive heat stress in summer. Surrounded by pollution generated by thousands of vehicles each day, they must cope with a variety of toxins. As impermeable surfaces rapidly drain away rainwater, they must survive periodic drought. Night and day they must endure foot traffic of a steady stream of pedestrians. Given the harshness of the urban environment, I expected to find few living things that would inhabit that world, but my explorations turned up far more than I would have guessed. Life abounds—even in cities.

I searched Front Street (our main downtown street) on many scales: microscopic, minute-but-visible, small-and-plain-to-see, and large-but-often-ignored. Bypassing microscopic, I examined minute-but-visible things first: those organisms lying low in joints of sidewalks or colonizing stone or masonry. In a short time I scratched up a black filmy lichen (I believe) and moss plants from a joint in the sidewalk. Too deep to be trod on by pedestrians, they grew out of a thin layer of black soil which had formed as organic matter somehow drifted into this tiny world. Even after a week of no rain, it was moist there—water was not a problem for tiny plants and the fungus that attend them. I wondered what microscopic animals lived with them, unseen by me—mites or tardigrades, perhaps.

The surfaces of concrete and stone provide another unlikely place for minute-but-visible living things. Vertical walls were barren, but horizontal ones showed abundant life. One of my favorites is a crustose lichen called *Caloplaca feracissima*, which might appear orange or rusty. It puts up little spore-bearing disks (apothecia) which are a treasure to look at under a ten-power lens. Another crustose lichen was visible under my lens appearing black with no apothecia. I was lucky to see any lichens, given the fact they are intolerant of pollution.

The small-and-plain-to-see category offered a wide display of living things. Among the weeds, purslane, prostrate spurge, and crab grass appeared frequently in less-traveled regions of the sidewalk, their flat, supine growth habit enabling them to occupy cracks without damage from passing foot traffic. Mostly dwarfed by harsh growing conditions, they would not flower and set seed—but wait! One abandoned purslane growing close to a building was gigantic and was about to flower. With luck it would set seed for the next generation. All of these plants had to start out from individual seeds that had somehow made it to downtown, but how did they get here? From shoes of passersby, soil in hanging pots of flowers, the wind? Imagine the tortuous pathways that resulted in a tiny plant growing in a crack in the sidewalk, but then—isn't it equally as amazing to consider the pathways we followed to occupy our own niche in time and space? Are we so different from the purslane struggling to survive in a cascade of footfalls?

Large-but-often-ignored animals include pigeons and gulls. Though occasional Herring gulls can be seen, Ring-bill gulls dominate the scavenger niche in Traverse City, out-competing crows by far. They are first on the scene when popcorn spills out or an ice cream cone is dropped on the sidewalk. I am delighted they can convert the junk food they eat into gorgeous white feathers. From time to time I find one on the street and take it home to pay it honor on my windowsill.

Pigeons are full-time residents of Traverse City. Our flock has about 35 individuals, that number not changing significantly over the years I have been here. In horse-and-buggy days there must have been much spilled grain that fell from wagons and at the doors of flour mills, but now food must be more scarce for pigeons, rats, and other animals that live off wastes of human consumption. The local flock spends some time at McGough's, a store near downtown that carries grains and seeds in bulk. Apparently, spilled grain on the parking lot in summer and winter attracts their interest. That nourishment must supply them with sufficient energy to conduct aimless flights around the downtown area, bombing runs that cover roofs, cars, and sidewalks with white splatters. Though many people are bothered by pigeon excrement, I value the birds' collective existence, especially in winter when the going is tough. How do they survive until spring? Does flying about aimlessly in winter help them out? I do not know.

House sparrows perch on Asian pear trees city officials have planted along Front Street. Like gulls, they, too, enjoy treats dropped by human passersby. One of them, I noticed, had discovered a more nutritious source of food. It would fly between the bars of the grill at the front of certain automobiles and come out with something in its beak. Of course! It was a dead insect that collided with the car at some faraway place. Animals exploit food sources wherever they are.

At all scales plants and animals, fungi and lichens occupy niches in Northern Michigan as exotic as those in the Amazon. The feeding relationships, the social relationships, the relationships that come about through accident, all contribute to their survival. Here is a haiku that tells about an unlikely connection between two crows. No doubt, the described action contributed to the survival of both of the birds.

he feeds her
a popcorn kernel...
crows of winter!

Hitchhiker in a wash basin

Having lived in an unheated shack with a wooden screen door the only barrier between me and the outside, I have encountered plenty of creatures as potential house-mates. Mice, bats, and chipmunks come to mind, as well as a host of insects and spiders. We treat each other with respect, but I kindly show them the door, bidding them good day and asking them to keep out, an admonition they seldom obey. One of them, a wee beast no longer than a quarter of a fingernail, dwells in my memory because of its curious appearance.

It possesses two sharply pointed pedipalps—resembling pincers—that extend from its head. It moves about on eight legs like a spider and displays a rounded abdomen, very different from the jointed tail of a scorpion with its stinger. I had seen it before, when I took a field course called "Biology of the Terrestrial Invertebrates." Students were asked to place leaf litter into galvanized steel funnels equipped with a screen at the narrow end. An incandescent bulb (now rarely seen) radiated heat and light onto the decaying leaves, sticks, moss, and fungus of the litter. Small animals migrated away from the unpleasant stimulus and dropped through the screen into a collecting jar. There were numberless insect-like springtails, spiders, millipedes, and centipedes. One of them stood out because it seemed to offer a threat to my extended finger: the *pseudoscorpion* described above. Lest the reader begin to panic, the beast is harmless to humans, apparently disinterested in biting us or else incapable of doing so. It feeds on arthropods smaller than itself—mites, springtails, ants—and will go after things that do us harm—clothes moth larvae, for one—so it should be considered a friend.

One day I saw a pseudoscorpion in a lavatory sink. After marveling at its shape and behavior—eventually setting it free in on forest leaf litter outside—I began to wonder how it got there. Certainly, with those tiny legs, it would not have crawled in through the door, up the plumbing, and then slid down the sink in an ecstasy of joy: that was just too much work for such a tiny thing.

Upon consulting recent research, I came upon the answer: it had hitched a ride on a flying insect, most likely a fly. Pseudoscorpions are known to grab onto the leg of a fly and take off with it for the fun of the ride, for evolutionary advantage, or by pure accident. There is a word for this sort of behavior: *phoresis* (or, *phoresy*). It turns out that pseudoscorpions (along with mites) are the hitchhikers of the microworld. Is it their restless natures that compel them to do this sort of behavior or do they gain something precious in exchange for their daring-do?

Phoresis is done for a variety of reasons. It can help a wee creature get away from a habitat soon to disappear, as when frost threatens a formerly livable habitat. It can enable a species to colonize new ground, as my washbasin pseudoscorpion tried to do. Or, on occasion, it can transport an animal to new food sources—even the very animal that is carrying it away. Certain pseudoscorpions do that very thing: eat the airplane that has been good enough to provide the ride.

We humans unwittingly carry animals to new places, too. For example, eyelash mites (genus *Demodex*) travel from person to person whenever we come into contact (pressing eyebrow to eyebrow is probably not a good idea). They were thought to be completely harmless, but now are regarded as parasitic, though they do not raise much havoc with most of us—a rash at most. Considering they inhabit nearly half of older adults and a third of younger folks, they cannot be called a dangerous pathogen since they do not make us sick. Whether it is humans with their mites or flies with their pseudoscorpions, hitchhiking is just another way animals take advantage of any mechanism that helps them survive. As Darwin taught us, adaptation is a fundamental principle of nature.

Here is a poem about the normal dwelling place of pseudoscorpions, the leaf litter:

the leaves below

Brown the brittle hulks around,
scrapes the one upon the other.
Veins spread upon their wrinkled faces thus:
images of the tree that gave them birth.

Descend to the cave below,
dark and dark again and still.
Here they do not scream
as pseudoscorpion's practiced fangs pierce the outer shell.
Here the sun does never shine,
where green is faded brown, and pallid fungi
extend their clammy fingers all around.

Hobo grasses of the prairie

One day many years ago, I set out on a botanizing expedition to the railroad tracks near my home. The place looked interesting, a swale that ended at the shore of a small lake, upland with oaks and blueberries, the lakeshore with— well, I didn't know for sure. I don't remember exactly what turned up there, but a human relic ended up being the most interesting of all: a circle of rocks surrounding a fire pit with a rusted can disintegrating nearby. Later, in my historical research, I learned the area was a hobo "jungle," a place where hobos would jump off the train just before it reached the railroad yard. It was a relatively safe place to make the leap since their transportation was compelled to slow down before entering the bustling area. And it was well-wooded in case the sheriff was bent on locking them up for a night or two on the charge of vagrancy, a crime that criminalized not having a fixed job or a home. Pursuit in a woods gives an advantage to the pursued.

Hobos were a diverse lot: old and young, intelligent or not, sober or alcoholic, slothful or industrious. Some came to my town to work the cherry and apple orchards, working harder than many of the townspeople who were critical of their appearance and the defects of moral character often falsely associated with unclean fingernails, greasy hair, ragged clothes, and unshaven faces. After the harvest workers hopped another freight to head for new destinations, most of them in warmer climes. Winter could be hard on the homeless in Northern Michigan.

Besides hobos, trains brought other accidental travelers, plant seeds from distant places. Though often failing to grow either because of unsuitable conditions or bad luck, sometimes they succeeded spectacularly. Unlike hobos, they would tarry alongside the tracks, putting down roots wherever they could. Grasses of the prairie did well when transported to sunny locations in Michigan that—but for white settlement—would have grown trees, pines on sandy soil, hardwoods on well-drained soil with more clay, and a host of conifers in mucky wetlands. With the coming of the railroads, trees were knocked back everywhere the tracks went, and roadbeds were raised above muck and sterile sand. Railroads converted forests into narrow fingers of prairie, the grasses and weeds of that ecosystem flourishing next to the rails. It helped that trains emitted cinders that often started wildfires, an important factor in the maintenance of grasslands.

Michigan offers little in terms of natural prairies. Near Kalamazoo, there is an ecosystem described as "oak openings," a name that hints at the sunny expanses of the grasslands further west. Too, the sandy shores of the Great Lakes support prairie grasses as winds and sterile soil tipped the balance towards grasses. Still, the state was mostly wooded from the state line in the south to the southern shore of Lake Superior. Grasses could not compete in a forest ecosystem with its dense canopy blocking the sun above and its thick layer of leaf litter preventing seed germination below.

Trains no longer travel on the tracks that carried hobos to Traverse City. The rails are rusted, the ties rotting, the roadbeds sinking into soil, the forlorn monuments with "W" (for 'whistle') engraved on them falling over or covered with graffiti. But amid the ruins of a long-gone age, prairie grasses remain—not only surviving, but flourishing, daring to grow between the ties, a fool's choice when trains were still running. Big bluestem, the most impressive species, stands seven feet tall, a beautiful blue flush of color at its joints (later turning reddish brown). It ripples in the wind as it did in Iowa two hundred years ago, before settlers set out to replace it with corn and soybeans. Before the plow turned prairie sod, big bluestem and its associate little bluestem fed enormous herds of buffalo throughout much of the West. Now its role is much reduced, much to the detriment of Midwestern soil and water resources, which were guarded by the extensive root systems of the grasses. For me, living in Northern Michigan, its austere flowers tell of the end of summer and the beginning of fall. Like the bright leaves of sugar maple, its drying stalks in the September sun mark the passage of time and the beginning of a new season.

Native and invasive species threaten prairie grasses growing along abandoned railroad tracks. Near my former hobo jungle, staghorn sumac, trembling aspen, and the foreigner Ailanthus are creeping closer to them, blocking the sun and stealthily converting this sunny grassland into Northern Michigan forest. I shouldn't worry too much about the loss of big and little bluestem, however. They have been introduced naturally or by design along the interstate highways, their medians and margins kept free of woody plants that might offer resistance to incursions of motor vehicles. Long fingers of the prairie will extend throughout Michigan along roads rather than railroad tracks. In any case, big bluestem and little bluestem, former hobos of the rails, are here to stay.

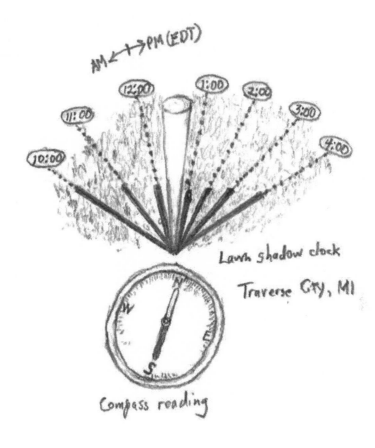

AM ←↑→ PM (EDT)

12:00 1:00 2:00
11:00   3:00
10:00   4:00

Lawn shadow clock

Traverse City, MI

Compass reading

How high the sun?

When is the sun is highest in the sky? I used to think it was 12:00 noon, a common misunderstanding among people. After all, there is the expression "high noon," an expression suggesting the sun is at its highest point at 12 o'clock. Upon reflection, it cannot be that time for everyone because we live at different places in our time zone, some more westerly than others. Those of us who live farthest east will see the sun at its highest point first, before the others living west of them.

In this day of easy internet access, it is not difficult to determine when the sun reaches its highest point: Get the astronomical information for a city, sun rise and set times, as well as the total hours of daylight for a given day. Traverse City, Michigan, recently gave these figures for one February day:

Sunrise 7:43 AM
Sunset 6:12 PM
Length of day: 10hr 29min

Dividing the number of daylight hours by two, you get about 5 hours, 14 minutes. Adding that to the sunrise time, it appears that the sun reaches its halfway point between rising and setting at 12:57 PM, a far cry from 12:00 noon.

Here is data from June 5:

Sunrise 5:59 AM
Sunset: 9:25 PM
Length of day: 15 hours, 24 minutes

Making the same calculations as before, the sun reaches its high point at 1:54 PM, a reasonable result given the time change from Eastern Standard Time (EST) to Eastern Daylight Time (EDT). It seems that the sun is at its highest point at approximately the same time. Readers of this book can get sunrise and sunset information from their own sources to determine "high (not) noon" for their own locality.

What practical importance does this have? First, if you use the sun as a compass, the shadows of things are at their shortest when the sun is highest in the sky. At that moment they point due north in all seasons: spring, summer, fall, or winter. When navigating in the woods without a GPS, it is good to remember that the sun reaches its highest point later in the afternoon.

In northern Michigan, there is another practical consequence to our late noon: an evening twilight that lasts well into the night. At the June solstice, there is light in the sky as late as 10 PM.

Another practical consideration has to do with the hottest time of the day. A thermal lag occurs between the time of greatest insolation (solar radiation) and the peak temperature observed for a given day. Ordinarily, the lag is about two hours after "high noon," which is, as we have said, about 1:54 PM in summer. That means the hottest temperature of the day would be about 4:00 PM, given no changes in the air mass or cloud cover over the area. Workouts would be less stressful at 12:00 noon rather than later in the afternoon.

Never one to avoid an opportunity to play with new understandings, I went to the internet to find a place that had its "moment in the (high) sun" closer to noon. Bangor, Maine, seemed like a good spot:

Sunrise: 4:50 AM
Sunset: 8:17 PM
Length of day, 15 hours, 27 minutes.

For this date (June 5, 2021) Bangor, Maine, had the sun reach its zenith at 12:47 PM EDT, a far cry from ours at 1:54 PM. It is much farther to our east in the Eastern time zone, and that makes the difference.

Every place on a local meridian has about the same time for its "high noon" (a meridian is a great circle that goes through the north and south poles), providing it is not too greatly separated in latitude (above the arctic circle the sun never sets in high summer). More simply, every location on the same longitude line has the same time of high noon. If I could find two well-known cities both at the same longitude (with a latitude not far different), then I could check to see if the sun reached its highest point at the same hour and minute. It turns out that Detroit, Michigan, and Columbus, Ohio, lie very close to longitude line 83 W: Would they have the same noon? Indeed, they do: 12:47 PM (approximately) for both of them. The two places may harbor college football teams with nasty attitudes towards each other, but the sun reaches its high point at the same time all year long.

Finally, now making sense of the sun's journey across the sky, I determined it was time to test that understanding with observations. On February 21, a bright sunny day, I plunked a stake vertically into the snow near my house: it looked vertical, anyway, ninety degrees to the ground. Then I made four observations:

10:30 AM	Shadow length, 58 inches (1.45 m)
12:57 PM	Shadow length 40 inches (1.00 m)
1:40 PM	Shadow length 41 inches (1.02 m)
2:50 PM	Shadow length 45 inches (1.13 m)

I stopped with these observations, since it was clear the shadow would keep lengthening as the day progressed. After measuring the height of the stake—it was 28 inches (.7 m)—I could find the tangent of the angle cast by the shadow when the sun was at its highest point. On this day in February, the tangent was .7000, that value giving an angle of 35 degrees, the same angle between the sun and the horizon on that day. On June 18th, near the time of the summer solstice, I measured the length of my own shadow: 31 inches (.78 m). Since I am six feet tall (in shoes and hat!), I get a value of 72/31 or 2.32 for the tangent of the angle. The table of tangents tells me that the sun is 66 degrees above the horizon on that day, a vast change from the freezing days of winter. Because early publication of this book disallows me to make observations on the winter solstice, I turn to NOAA's calculator at https://gml.noaa.gov/grad/solcalc/azel.html. For Traverse City's coordinates, the predicted value of the sun's height is about 22 degrees above the horizon. I look forward to testing that prediction on a cold December day in the future.

I hope readers will determine the time the sun reaches its highest point in their locality, not just to satisfy scientific curiosity, but to anchor one's self in a particular time and space. Inquiry begins locally, asking questions about things in plain sight, and proceeds to generalizing about what is learned, then finding out more with further research. That is the sort of science Galileo, Newton, and Darwin did, and it is a good model to follow even now.

The cycle of long and short days is ingrained in our beings. The longest day is celebrated at the summer solstice, and the dawn of longer days to come is celebrated at the winter solstice. Solstice is a time of joy and heightened expectations for all, especially those connected to the agricultural season. This poem tells about shortened days and the feelings engendered by them:

When November Comes

When the sun falls so short of the sky's center,
And the shadows are long at noon,
When the electric wires shine in the mid-day sun
And bare branches glow against the darkening day,
When the north wind offers no hope of warmth
And the diving ducks return to the river,
When the morning glories sway brown against the snow
And the chirp of the cricket is heard no more
Then you will come and comfort me,
As I will you. And we shall live in a quiet home,
Nurturing the bountiful spring that dwells in us.

For the love of jumping spiders

Its jerky movements attracted my attention. On the screen door, a fairly large spider was searching for food, or else trying to get off the metallic matrix of wires on which it found itself. Not particularly afraid of spiders, I bent over to study it carefully and saw that its "jaws" were turquoise blue!

It was a jumping spider, one I had seen before as a (somewhat maladjusted) teenager. Back then, as I bent over to look at it more carefully, it jumped on me, causing me to cuff wildly to get it off. Now, in the more rational years of my adulthood, I am capable of studying the spider close-up, even bringing out my lens to get a better look.

What attracts my attention is its eyes. Like most spiders, it has eight of them, but the two in front are large and placed side-by-side, like ours. They are not the unmoving compound eyes of dragonflies, but limpid pools that stare at you. If you move something in one direction, the spider will orient itself to follow the movement. What is it seeing, exactly?

Much research has been done about jumping spider vision. Unlike us, they can sense polarized light, like that scattered in a blue sky. That is one way they learn about the time of day and their location in relation to the sun. Like us, they can see color—no reds—but ultraviolet as compensation. They can tell distance, too, through an elaborate system that processes green wavelengths at two different levels in the retina. By getting information from two levels, they can compare the fuzziness of one image to the sharpness of the other, thereby determining the distance.

Knowing how far away a juicy insect prey is, the jumping spider can perform its leaps with great accuracy. How far can they leap? Far enough to surprise a young thirteen-year-old boy many years ago. Eight or nine inches (20 cm) are not unheard of. Before leaping, they fasten a safety line of silk to their substrate. If necessary, they can reel themselves back up after an unsuccessful attack.

Jumping spiders seem more intelligent than most insects. Perhaps it's those eyes. If you look carefully into its large medial eyes, you can see movement of some kind. The spider is unable to move its eyes in its sockets as we can, but it can move its retina so it can follow the movement of prey.

For the love of jumping spiders

But what does a jumping spider actually see? How does it perceive the world? While aiming his camera towards an insect, an investigator took a photograph through the lense of a spider's eye. (I am sorry to report the spider had to have been killed.) Clear images of the insect could be obtained at the proper focal distance. It appears that it can see images at a distance of eight or nine inches, a distance consistent with its jumping ability.

One should never pass up the opportunity to play with creatures like jumping spiders. A mirror held up to a male can sometimes elicit threatening postures, as it perceives a possible rival for a mate. Videos of male rivals on an iPhone screen can elicit such responses, too. By the way, in general, jumping spiders do not have the ability or interest to bite us: they prefer smaller, more tasty organisms.

We humans are arrogant when it comes to evaluating the intelligence of other creatures. In all matters we imagine we are kings of the hill. In fact, though, our intelligence is highly overrated. I would like to see any human capture a single insect prey as skillfully as a jumping spider. Within its domain of insect predation, it is far more intelligent than we are.

The hills are alive

Recently I learned that hills "creep." That is, that if they are left on their own, they gradually subside, presumably in the far future disappearing altogether. Gravity drives the collapse, and diminished friction between soil particles caused by soaking rains hastens the process. Old stone walls that hold back soil give evidence of this phenomenon: they begin to lean away from the hills that back them up, eventually toppling over altogether.

In my town I knew the perfect place to observe the creeping of hills, a place settled perhaps a hundred years before the time I made my observations. A stout stone wall surrounded an estate which had seen better days, as one might infer from the state of decay of the masonry. In some places the wall held back a hill, while in others it stood on its own, not holding back anything. Could I see the creep of the hill from the leaning of the wall? And would I see any difference between sections of the wall that had to resist hill creep vs. those that didn't? Equipped with a simple plumb bob made of a weight on a string, I went out to test the lean of the wall at two different places.

Where the hill backed up to the wall, the bob revealed considerable lean—perhaps ten degrees, I estimated. By contrast, the sections of the wall standing free showed no lean at all. Not only that, but a wide crack had opened in the wall that separated the two sections. Apparently mere stone and concrete cannot resist the force of gravity pushing the wall over. If not attended to promptly, the compromised wall would topple within a decade or two. It appeared the hill was creeping, and that no wall could stop it.

One way to slow down creeping is a cover of vegetation that anchors soil grains and prevents washouts. A leaf cover over the ground helps, too, as it enables rain to penetrate slowly, rather than all at once, but sometimes the slow work of centuries happens in a moment. A four-inch (10 cm) rain can convert soil into a slurry that suddenly slumps into valleys. Such dramatic changes in the land occur more frequently than we might guess. Two hundred years ago, geologists were convinced that the process of erosion occurred at a slow pace, literally one grain of soil at a time. Now we know rapid, catastrophic events are the rule rather than the exception. Hills may creep, but they also wash out.

With all this subsidence, it is a fair question to ask where hills come from in the first place. Where I live, they were plastered onto the landscape by a continental glacier that extended over the land some 8000 years ago. Moraines are the relics of rocks and soil scraped up by the ice as it advanced southward. Some of them stand hundreds of feet high as the melting ice left great piles of mixed sand, gravel, and rock.

Besides glaciers, there is another way hills are formed, especially in areas close to the edge of the Great Lakes: sand dunes. Though dunes and moraines may look alike if they are forested, it is easy to tell them apart. Rocks—boulders, cobbles, or pebbles—are found on moraines but not on dunes, since the latter are heaps of wind-blown sand. In my town there are both landforms.

I visit a moraine to look for wildflowers in the spring. The soil, laden with rocks and a mixture of clay and sand, is a perfect habitat for Trillium and Jack-in-the-pulpits. Another hill nearby reveals itself as a dune. Residential construction has exposed the soil underneath—pure sand. Covered with oaks, pines, and poison ivy, it has a different forest from the first. There can be no doubt: it is a dune masquerading as a moraine. Not all dunes are active, open to the ravaging of the wind. Some attain old age and just sit there, creeping a bit over time, but never revealing their origin. That is the way this one was.

Hills creep. They also collapse in landslides. Except for such catastrophic events, we are unaware of the pace of change, but the walls we build to hold back the hills let us know what we are missing as they age and begin to lean. At all timescales, nature makes the final decisions.

The hills are alive

Here is haiku about pace of change and how we perceive it.

> *how rapid the flow of hills!*
> *how slow the flight of dragonflies!*
> *so we pass our lives...*

The sound of poplars

I suffer from Meniere's disease, a condition that, in my case, affects both ears. While the vertigo associated with it is no longer a problem, continual tinnitus and hearing loss trouble me throughout my days and nights. Several years ago, I received a cochlear implant which restored my hearing—to an extent. While most people—even those with more tractable hearing loss—have untold thousands of hearing receptors covering a wide range of frequencies, I am faced with a much reduced ability to sense tones and overtones. It is like being given a tiny box of eight crayons of different colors rather than a grand box of sixty-four. Eight crayons are better than none, and yet....

A cochlear implant, while greatly limited in responding to different frequencies, responds well to percussion and repetitive loud noises. The sounds of construction next door, with its constant hammering, come through clearly, much to my exasperation. Motorcycles and helicopters are painfully loud, the pulses of sound causing me to shield my ears with my hands. While those individual explosions of artificial sound are especially annoying, there is one sound of nature that comes through clearly, perhaps more clearly than I remember in the days of good hearing: the sounds of crickets and other such insects.

Crickets have a file on one outer wing and a scraper on the other. When they rub together, the characteristic chirp is produced—like running a fingernail across the teeth of a comb. For me, that method of producing sound is perfect: tiny explosions, one after another. A long drawn out note that a violin might make, or an opera diva might sing sounds like a howl to me—much to my sorrow, since I used to enjoy those sounds.

Another natural sound that attracts my interest is the voice of wind in the trees. Poplar leaves tremble in the wind, the slightest breeze pushing unequally on the two halves of the leaf, the flattened leaf stem pulling one side back when the twist is too great (or so it looks to me). When they strike against each other rapidly, the percussive effect is deafening to my ears: It is as if an audience of thousands were all clapping their hands together. Larger oak leaves do not respond as quickly as poplars, and their signature applause has a different tonal quality. The whistling of the wind through pine needles I scarcely notice.

There is a word for the sound of the wind in the trees: *psithurism*, a word that comes from ancient Greek referring to the act of whispering. Though rarely used nowadays, the word is applied to the rustling of leaves in the wind. Presumably, in ancient times, people were more attuned to that nearly omnipresent sound. In that long-gone world of natural sounds, psithurism was as common as traffic noise is today. It anchored human consciousness to the wind and the weather, just as the sounds of the modern world remove us from it. We must open ourselves to nature again if we are to recover what we have lost.

Psithurism did not escape the notice of Emily Dickensen:

The Wind

Of all the sounds despatched abroad,
There's not a charge to me
Like that old measure in the boughs,
That phraseless melody

The wind does, working like a hand
Whose fingers brush the sky,
Then quiver down, with tufts of tune
Permitted gods and me.

The sound of poplars

When winds go round and round in bands,
And thrum upon the door,
And birds take places overhead,
To bear them orchestra,

I crave him grace, of summer boughs,
If such an outcast be,
He never heard that fleshless chant
Rise solemn in the tree,

As if some caravan of sound
On deserts, in the sky,
Had broken rank,
Then knit, and passed
In seamless company.

Remembering my perception of sound, I offer this haiku:

in celebration of the wind
they clap with all their might
trembling aspen leaves!

49

Finally, I will not leave the subject of soundscape without pointing to something that surrounds all sounds: silence. We only pay attention to sounds, forgetting the fertile context of silence that gives rise to them. As the spaces between letters and words give text meaning, so does omnipresent silence make the world come alive. The *Tao Te Ching* says it this way:

> *Great sound is silent*
> *Great form is shapeless.*
> *The Tao is hidden and nameless;*
> *Yet it alone knows how to render help and to fulfill.*

Sun leaves and shade leaves

When I was beginning to learn the names of trees, I was often confused by the lack of correspondence between pictures of leaves displayed in guidebooks and the shapes of the actual leaves, themselves. Oaks were especially bothersome, especially the black oak *(Quercus velutina)*. That species was supposed to have deeply incised leaves, but often had nothing more than notches. In time I came to understand that leaves can differ in shape and size according to their position on the tree. Leaves at the top are regarded as typical, and take on the shape indicated in the

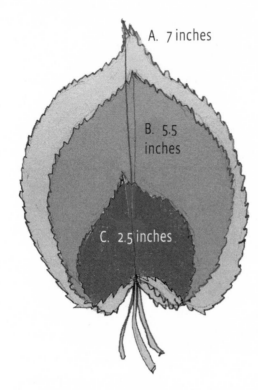

A. 7 inches

B. 5.5 inches

C. 2.5 inches

Basswood leaves
(Tilia americana)

Relative sizes
Measurements reflect real values

A. juvenile leaves of sprouts
B. shade leaf
C. sun leaf

Metric equivalents:
7 inches = 17.5 cm
5.5 inches = 13.8 cm
2.5 inches = 6.3 cm

guidebooks. They are usually much smaller than the ones lower down, those that are shaded by the canopy above. I measured a shade leaf of an American basswood *(Tilia americana)*, with the blade about five inches in width and 5.5 inches in length—in contrast to a leaf exposed to the sunlight—with measurements 2.5 inches by 3 inches. Less spectacularly, a black oak shade leaf measured 5.5 inches by 7.5, with the corresponding measurements in the sun leaf coming in at 5.5 by 4.5. (See diagram above for metric equivalents.) Unlike the basswood, the two leaves of the oak were vastly different in shape, the sun leaves greatly incised. Why should leaves on the same tree look so different both in size and shape?

Sun leaves and shade leaves

Trees make different leaves so they can maximize the use of sunlight in order to carry on photosynthesis. Leaves at the top of the tree are more tightly packed with photosynthetic cells compared to those at the bottom. They intercept more of the sun's rays, thereby enabling the plant to make more food. Leaves at the bottom of the tree have wider areas, and are able to capture more patches of sunlight that strike them as the wind blows the upper canopy about. Though larger in area, they are typically thinner, with a narrower band of photosynthetic cells. To a tree intent on growing as fast as possible, it all makes sense.

I am less certain why the shapes of leaves vary so widely, especially in oaks. There must be a difference in genetic expression, with shade leaves being arrested in a more juvenile stage. In contrast to oaks, many trees show little difference in sun and shade leaves; lower poplar leaves look like the upper ones in a mature tree, though that characteristic could be explained by the scant shade provided by the canopy. Maples show some difference in size, though the shape of the leaves stays the same. Trees with compound leaves also show about the same, top and bottom.

One factor seldom commented on is that tendency of the upper leaves to lose chlorophyll first in the fall, well before the lower leaves. It is as if they simply grow tired of photosynthesizing all summer long and give up before the first frost. More reasonably, the sun's rays, though necessary for life, are also quite destructive to enzymes, and to chlorophyll itself. The bright red of the top of a maple in late September contrasts nicely with the summer green of the lower leaves. Is that yet another way trees can maximize photosynthesis— enabling the lower leaves to finally have their day in the sun? Perhaps.

Besides their position in the canopy, there is another way leaves can differ in size and shape. With some tree species, young leaves can become gigantic in comparison to adult leaves. The young off-shoots at the base of basswoods have leaves like that. I measured one with a blade of 7 inches by 5.5 inches, its area far bigger than shade leaves or sun leaves. Juvenile black oak leaves, while not spectacular in size, show the same differences in shape that the shade leaves do. Young black poplar leaves can be grotesquely different from those of the parent trees. One young shoot had lower young leaves that were five times bigger in area than those towards the top of the stem. A trembling aspen *(Populus tremuloides)* growing nearby showed no such irregularity.

No wonder my tree identification books led me astray as I labored through descriptions of the different species that live in my neighborhood. Leaves can be as fickle as the weather in how they present themselves. Though it seems like artful capriciousness, they have their own reasons for doing so. Nature does not mock us, although it may confound us.

Sun leaves and shade leaves

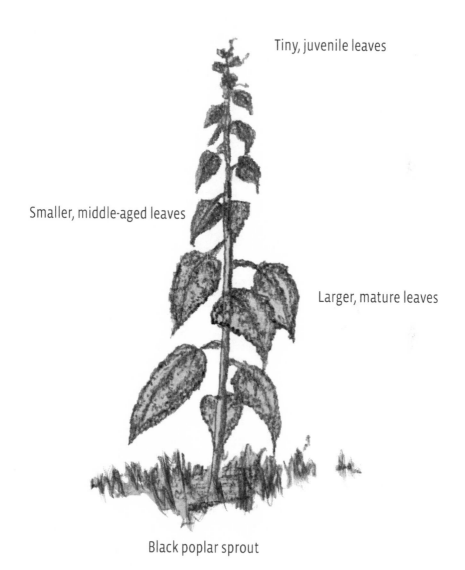

Tiny, juvenile leaves

Smaller, middle-aged leaves

Larger, mature leaves

Black poplar sprout

Missing half the world: the sky in day and night

In the absence of trees and buildings, half of our visual field is comprised of the sky. Out West, where trees are often absent, arriving settlers called the region the "Big Sky Country," taking note of the panorama an unobstructed sky lays before us. In the East we are less likely to pay attention to its transformations: the gathering of clouds before a storm, the fleeting appearance of rainbows, the clearing afterwards, sunrises and sunsets, the coming of twilight, and the fullness of resplendent night with its stars and planets as well as the changing face of the moon.

Missing half the world: the sky in day and night

Though we are diurnal creatures that treasure the hours of light, we leave the natural world behind for half our lives—much to our spiritual loss. Omnipresent artificial lights blast the night sky away, so little regard we have to preserve it.

It is hard to imagine life before artificial lighting. As the sun set, the stars would come out (or not), the moon would illuminate the landscape (or not), occasional meteors would shoot across the sky, the planets would come together in their march along the ecliptic, and a comet would appear every few decades. The night could not be escaped by means of electronic entertainment watched indoors. With all its wonder (and its terror), the sky gave structure to our lives as it dictated our waking and sleeping hours. Now we must make a conscious effort to return to the natural cycle of day and night as we abandon clock time for sun time. While modern life forbids most of us from making so drastic a change, we can simply look up more often during day and night. We can direct our attention away from human things, and towards the everlasting verities of the sky.

When we wake up to the sky, we first notice clouds. On fair weather days white puffs of cumulus decorate the blue, some of them building quite high before they begin to collapse. Hawks know them well for they signal rising air and a free ride in the updraft. Sometimes two dozen or more will circle beneath them in a tight column, a kettle of hawks. They may break away and glide for a time to the base of a nearby cloud and ride the wind up again, a carnival ride free of the necessity of flapping wings to keep aloft. Cumulus clouds are a joy to all beings.

The coming of a storm is often foretold by clouds. In the mid-latitudes, the prevailing wind is from the west, and that is the direction to look if you wish to learn about the weather to come. After weeks of drought, I see a high deck of clouds in the southwest, touches of wispy cirrus clouds, then a thin deck of altostratus, the layer getting thicker as it touches the horizon. A storm is on the way, and I hope it reaches here soon. In twelve hours or so, I will know.

With the storm often comes lightning, and it is worth our while to wait for its strike, and to count the seconds until thunder roars. The difference between the near-instantaneous arrival of flash and the later arrival of the sound explains the general rule that a five second delay indicates a distance of approximately a mile (three seconds per kilometer). Lightning can be within a cloud, between clouds, or cloud to ground, so it is not clear that a devastating strike occurred nearby if there is little delay between flash and roar. Even so, it is best to seek shelter in a storm rather than stand close to isolated trees and towers, nor is it safe to stand alone in a barren field.

After the worst of the rain—if we are lucky—we might see a rainbow. We need to stand with our backs to the sun and look outward, ever hoping the sun will illuminate falling raindrops in our field of view. Owing to physical principles of dispersion, refraction and reflection, a bow will describe an arc of 42 degrees from the sun, but, because of the interference of the ground, we cannot see the whole circle. The closer the sun is to the horizon, the wider the rainbow will appear. Those about noontime will be low in the sky, but those nearing sunrise and sunset will arc high above the ground. Always the sky enclosed by the primary rainbow will appear brighter than that above it, an observation often ignored by viewers so transfixed they are by the display of color. Sometimes a secondary bow can be seen with the colors reversed, red on the inside.

Missing half the world: the sky in day and night

Besides rainbows, other sky phenomena present themselves to us, many of them ignored because we avoid looking towards the sun. Crepuscular rays shoot out from gaps in clouds that obscure the sun's disk after sunrise or before sunset. They appear to converge at the sun's location, an optical illusion akin to the apparent merging of two parallel railroad tracks viewed by an observer standing between them. Halos are circles of light that appear at 22 degrees from the sun, the space covered by your hand held at arm's length. They are caused by high-altitude ice crystals that bend and reflect sunlight, often presenting rainbow effects. Iridescent clouds display swatches of rainbow colors, but are often missed in the glare of a winter's sun. Sundogs, bright patches of light on either side of the sun, are observed at sunrise and sunset during the cold months, too. All of these phenomena are available to us if we take a moment to hold up our hand to block the sun's brightness. We avoid staring at the sun for good reason—to protect our eyes—but we can enjoy the show by seeking the shade of a nearby object while looking off to one side, out of the corner of our eyes. For a lover of nature, that simple gesture is more than a salutary health practice. It is a salutation to the beauty of sun and sky.

Nor should we forget the beauty of the night. As with the sun, halos around the moon can be seen, especially during the cold months when a thin layer of ice crystals forms high in the atmosphere. During warmer months, a layer of fog droplets, each of about the same size, can make a corona around the moon, the brightest part touching the moon's orb, while gradually fading at the reddish outer region. The glow is little different from the glow around street lamps in the fog; it only impresses us because we so seldom take the time to look up and enjoy moonlight. Taking that time is a salutation to the beauty of the moon and the night.

I close this chapter with one of my favorite verses from the *Rubaiyat* of Omar Khayyam. It could only have been written by a sage who took joy in the sun and stars.

> *Wake! For the Sun, who scatter'd into flight*
> *The stars before him from the Field of Night,*
> *Drives Night along with them from Heav'n, and strikes*
> *The Sultan's Turret with a Shaft of Light.*
> Translation by Edward Fitzgerald

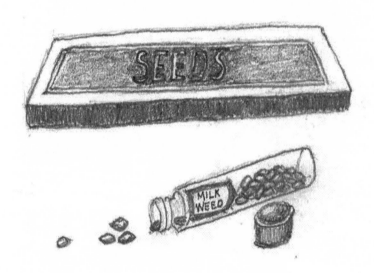

The seed collection

Cornelia's house is a treasure trove. Shelves are piled with books of every description, some going back to her childhood, which began 94 years ago. Rocks and minerals are laid out—moonstone, jasper, hematite, puddingstones, and Petoskeys. A magnet is suspended by a string from a kitchen cupboard, its purpose to determine the magnetic qualities of stones she picks up on Great Lakes beaches. Drawers and cabinets reveal sets of antique silverware, paper-cut artwork, complete sets of china, and table linens going back a hundred years ago or more. By her accustomed seat next to a window, her binoculars lie close at hand: she watches birds and squirrels with great interest and acumen. As soon as you enter her house, you step upon Oriental rugs that once adorned her grandparents' home.

I enter her home twice a week, on Thursday and Sunday, to play intense games of Scrabble. Until recently, Tucker, her 14-year-old Labrador retriever would announce my presence with thunderous barking. Her cat, Prince Albert, will make his appearance later, in a furtive effort to escape through the front door when I am on my way out. Now, since Tucker passed away, Prince Albert lounges next to the Scrabble board, his tail sometimes threatening the order of the game. Like Cornelia, he misses his friend.

One day a manuscript appeared beside the Scrabble board. Laboriously typed with few corrections on yellowing paper, it was about three pages long. My interest was attracted at once: MAKING A SEED COLLECTION it proclaimed in bold letters. Cornelia knew it would intrigue me, because she knows I taught biology for 31 years in the local school system, and because I have a special interest in plants. I had to read it before our game, and with her permission, did just that.

Making a seed collection

In my second year of high school, I was taking biology. Mr. Stanek, our teacher, required us to make a collection of some kind—insects, flowers, leaves, or anything pertaining to biology. We had about five weeks to do it in. Our class went on a field trip to the open fields out west of the city so that we might begin collecting our specimens. I remember how I wandered around from group to group, listening to them talking about this wonderful sunflower, or that queer grasshopper there, or this oddly shaped leaf. I couldn't make up my mind. I didn't like any of those collections. When we got home and school was over for the day, I went home and sat around the house moping. "Darn it! I don't know what to collect. I don't like biology anyway." My mother, sympathizing with me, told me about a collection she made in school. It was weed seeds. She might still have it around the house somewhere. Hum-m-m-m. There was an idea. She still had her collection?

Well, Mother searched for it, but couldn't find it. However, by that time I had grown interested in the subject of weed seeds and decided I might as well go ahead with it. Before getting any seeds, I thought I ought to have something to put them in. I went to several drug stores and asked for little bottles two or three inches high (5 – 7.5 cm). No, they didn't have any "phials," as I learned they were called. This was a pretty discouraging start. Nothing to put my seeds in. Just as I was ready to give up, I found a drug store that did have phials and that would sell them to me. It was a Whelan's. The man could sell me eight phials. That was better than none, but not enough. However, if one Whelan's had them, why not another? I rode my bike about four miles (6 km) to the next nearest Whelan's Drug Store and obtained enough phials to make my collection.

So far, so good. Now I had to fill them up. I never had so much fun while doing school work. I rode my bicycle all over the southwest side of town, where the country was open, and gathered my weeds and seeds.

The seed collection

I remember those long rides I took with my mother and the good times we had discussing various plants. Each name of a weed brings to my mind a picture of the place where I found it. We were gathering mustard seeds at 71st, and Leavitt when the streamliner rushed by on the tracks. I didn't go far to get pigweed seeds; they grew right in our alley alongside the church fence. It was on our way home from the airport that we found the bouncing betty. The sunflowers were in an empty lot near our house. Smartweed, I found, grows along the practically all the city sidewalks. It was at 85th and Kedzie that I found a field of blazing stars. Milkweed grew in the fields along Western Avenue. (We gathered several mildewed pods and left them in our back porch. Soon the floor looked as though it had snowed in there.)

I put all my seeds in bottle covers till I was ready to work with them. Then, the next problem was to separate the actual seeds from all the chaff that surrounded them. That was quite a task with certain weeds, and took a great deal of patience. But soon I was ready to put the seeds in the phials. I did this, one kind of seed at a time, and labeled the phial with sticky paper. I put them in a flat box, like a tie or glove box.

My collection was about done. I had one thing more to do, though— write a paper telling the dates I had gathered my seeds and places. That stumped me. I hadn't kept a record—or so I thought. Then I remembered my diary. I hadn't written that I had gathered a certain seed at such and such a place, but it did tell me where I had ridden and when. For instance, on October 8th—"I rode to the airport today with Mom… Stopped at a field near Kostner Avenue on the way home to get seeds." Well, I remembered we'd come home along 62nd, and I very definitely remembered getting stuck with all the thistles there. But I did get the seeds—Canadian thistles. In this way, I was able to make out my record. And when that was completed, I handed the collection in.

Mr. Stanek was delighted with it. He thought it was excellent. In fact, he liked it so well, that he put it on exhibit in the show window for a few days.

Writing, teacher's remarks: *A; Even weeds can be entertaining and useful if you know how to use them.*

"Neil, you saved this from when you were sixteen years old?" I asked when I had finished reading.

"Yes, it's been shut away someplace. I just came across it." She shrugged her shoulders as if realizing it was it bit odd for someone to keep a high school project that long.

"You cared about it so much, you never threw it away." As a former teacher, I love it when former students remember something they did in class.

"Mr. Stanek put it in the display case for students to look at," she said with pride.

"Mr. Stanek was a fine teacher. You wouldn't have kept this paper if he hadn't made an impression on you. I especially liked it that you and your mother worked together on it. It brought you together."

"She made a weed collection herself, years before. We went out on our bicycles to find weeds she recognized." There was evident joy in remembering her experience.

"You kept your interest in wildflowers and plants your whole life—remember when we would go out on wildflower expeditions to identify plants?"

She did remember. This biology project—along with her mother's earlier project on weeds—fed her love of plants and nature.

Our interchange triggered rambling reflections within me as a biology teacher.

I could not help but contrast Mr. Stanek's assignment with learning activities presented to students nowadays. Biology in 2021 is about grasping broad concepts like photosynthesis, respiration, and genetics. It seldom touches on local trees, weeds, or seeds. It is highly abstract with terms such as "ATP," "meiosis," and "the Krebs cycle," all printed in bold type, emphasizing the kind of learning expected in 16 year-olds. In my opinion, that is not totally wrong, but nor is it right. If local biology is sacrificed on the altar of Big Ideas, then something important is neglected.

Why did the knowledge of local plants and animals come to be devalued in high school biology? The chief reason is that standardized tests do not address such things. After all, test questions are designed to compare individuals, teachers, schools, school districts, and states. Knowing a maple leaf from an oak leaf has less importance than an understanding of "transpiration" or the meaning of "homologous chromosomes." The problem is that, if the level of abstraction goes up, many students are going to drop away in boredom and confusion. There is a trade-off between comprehension of Big Ideas and a possible lifelong interest in biology—at least for some students. In fact, we should demand both: the important concepts AND a knowledge of the biology around us.

After sharing a few of these thoughts with Neil, I returned to the business at hand: Scrabble. We split, each one of us winning one game. She had a "Bingo," as I recall—all seven tiles used at once for a bonus score of 50.

The next week she had a special surprise waiting for me: her seed collection! She brought out a long, red box, five inches wide and over a foot long (12.5 x 30 cm); a box she supposed that once contained cigarettes or small cigars. She'd covered over the maker's name with blue construction paper, and lined the border with a white paper frame. Prominently, the word "SEEDS" occupied the center of the field, each letter positioned in exactly the right place. It is no wonder she developed an interest in paper-cut art and origami later in her life.

I opened the box and looked inside. Twelve vials of seeds, each lettered on a red-bordered label, rolled about inside. My friend said almost apologetically, "My son got into it when he was young, and six of them are missing." I reassured her that didn't matter—the collection was splendid as it was. Attached to the inside of the lid were two long sheets of paper upon which were written the name of the weed, the closest street corner in Chicago where it was collected, and the date by month and day (presumably all were collected in 1940 when she was sixteen). Printed in black ink with a fine-pointed pen, every letter was formed precisely in a space not too far and not too close to its nearest neighbor. No wonder Mr. Stanek had displayed this box in his showcase! It was a beautifully done piece of work.

Neil and I began to speculate if the seeds would grow after all these years. The curly dock, wild mustard, sweet clover, burdock, smartweed, and all the rest—would they sprout after 79 years of storage in cupboards and elsewhere? I told her about the world's longest running experiment at Michigan State University in which botanist William Beal, in 1879, buried 20 inverted glass vessels containing a variety of weed seeds in soil on the school campus. (The up-side-down glasses kept out water.) Every five years—later that period was extended to ten and then twenty—a jar was dug out and the seeds were exposed to water for sprouting. A single hardy weed seed toughed it out in the 2000 opening, with a few more glasses remaining to be tested in coming years. We wondered: Would Neil's seeds germinate after 79 years in glass vials? I would contact Michigan State to see if anyone would want to find out the answer.

Not receiving a reply, I set out to do the experiment myself. Twenty seeds of each type were folded into moist paper toweling, each kind being inserted into plastic sandwich bags to prevent evaporation. Putting them a dark cupboard, I waited two weeks to see if any of them would sprout: My expectations were high.

Alas, after two weeks had passed, not one seed in any of the bags had shown any sign of life. While Cornelia had survived 79 years after they were harvested, the weed seeds had passed away years before, testimony to both the fragility of life and its endurance.

Willow and oak: a tale of two trees

The black willow that stood on the grounds of the former Traverse City State Psychiatric Hospital was magnificent. Its girth was 1,016 cm (33.3 ft), its diameter 323 cm (127 in), and its height 23.2 m (76 ft). For a time, it was the national champion black willow, the biggest of all trees measured of its species. Sadly, its condition has degraded since the time those measurements were taken—the figures quoted came from *Michigan Trees* by Burton Barnes and Warren Wagner, published in 1981. Today it is a decaying relic of its former self with a few shoots remembering the glory of its past. Not all trees live as long as redwoods.

Certainly, a tree of such size must have begun its life hundreds of years ago—national champion trees do not pop up overnight. Yet, it is worthwhile to look critically at the age of large trees. Some time ago, I looked at the 1850 surveyor records of this area, and found that the forest that occupied the grounds of this part of the State Hospital grounds was made up of black and white spruce, hemlock, white cedar and other trees of northern wetlands. Most likely it was a dense forest that allowed little sunlight to reach the ground; where young trees struggled to survive in continuous shade cast by the crowns of the conifers that grew all around. In such an environment, a single black willow sprout would have faced a tough journey in its path to adulthood—if, indeed, it started out in the forest at all. It may have begun after the forest was cleared by settlers, growing vigorously in land well-watered and cleared of competition from nearby trees. Perhaps it wasn't so old at all.

Traverse City was settled about 1850, its towering pines and oaks felled over the next thirty-five years. The Hospital (then called the Northern Michigan Asylum) was constructed in 1885, and its campus was cleared in the years immediately before that date. Suddenly, great opportunities appeared for a young black willow sprout that had struggled to overtop its conifer neighbors. With unfettered access to sunlight and water, its annual growth rings widened to a centimeter every year for hundred years, and, mercifully, in the shelter of a hill to the west, storms did not tip it over. It became a national champion tree, but—oddly—was not especially old. Three

factors accounted for its success: it was a fast-growing species; it was lucky; and, with its competitors removed, it had perfect growth conditions.

Free of competition from other trees, many species attain a large size at an early age. They are easy to recognize, even from a distance, as they are abundantly branched at levels close to the ground. City trees planted along streets take on this form, as do single trees planted in parks or along golf courses. Foresters call them "wolf trees," perhaps because they are lone wolves, separated from the pack. Essentially worthless for lumber, they still provide value in providing shade, branches with nesting places, and fruits for beasts both haired and feathered. Though spoiled brats in comparison to forest trees that must battle it out to get sunlight, they still enrich our lives beyond measure.

Traverse City has another fabled tree, much cherished by those who know it. On a residential street near the downtown, a giant white oak grows near the sidewalk with one of its branches curiously bent like an elbow. At its base a plaque is attached to a small boulder. Its inscription reads:

BEHOLD THIS TREE
BENT BY THE INDIANS
Guide Post on Trail
Detroit to Straits of Mackinaw

This memorial erected by
Grand Traverse Historical Society

It is not my purpose to investigate whether it was really "bent by the Indians," but rather to determine if the tree was old enough to have been bent in such a manner. Given that settlement and land clearing began about 1850, was the tree old enough to have been manipulated—presumably with a woven cord—at the time local Odawa and Ojibwe people traveled to Detroit and Mackinaw by following trail markers?

Lucius Lyon, a well-known surveyor, wrote of a stretch of land extending from roughly the position of present-day Eighth Street to Grand Traverse Bay: *Land nearly level, plain, sandy soil, poor, second-rate. White and Yellow (Red) Pine, White and Red Oak.* In the years following, the pines were promptly logged off, but many of the oaks remained: one of them, the famous trail-marker. One line of evidence is a photograph taken in 1895 that shows the tree in a famous citizen's front yard. It appears to be of moderate size even then, quite old, certainly older than forty years. Shaded by taller pines in its youth, it would have grown slowly to attain the girth it displayed at that time. I have examined cut stumps of trees compelled to compete for sunlight that were the size of a typical telephone pole, and counted sixty or more annual growth rings in the cross section. Each one was thinner than a dime in its earliest years. An age of 250 years would not be an exaggeration for this revered tree.

So it is that we have two trees, one a black willow growing in sunlight with abundant water, and the other a white oak competing for sunlight with neighboring pines. The first became a champion; the second, a revered, but unspectacular tree growing along a roadside street. Growing conditions and genetics explain how rapidly trees grow—large trees are not necessarily old, nor are small trees young. There is no tried-and-true rule. Nature is too complex for that.

Willow and oak: a tale of two trees

Maples and oaks: trees that hurry, trees that wait

How we take joy in the leafing out of trees in spring! Bare sticks become flag poles, twigs become alive with color. Maples, poplars, willows, and basswood push out their leaves on sunny days even when night temperatures fall below freezing. By the middle of May in Northern Michigan, they have created a canopy of leaves, the shade now overwhelming the forest wildflowers below. But there are laggards: Oaks, black walnut, black locust, and catalpa seem to be biding their time with their leaf buds still bound up into protective bud scales well into the month of May. What is one to make of these latecomers?

The answer to that question lies in the architecture of a tree's stem. Sap is conducted up from the roots through xylem tissue, loosely called wood. Every year a new ring of xylem is added as the tree increases in diameter. Maples, poplars, and all the rest of the trees first to leaf out can use xylem rings made the previous year as their plumbing is already in place. But laggard trees like oaks must make the effort to form a new xylem layer in the spring before it can begin to open its leaves. It takes time to grow the new layer, and that accounts for the late development of leaves.

What is different about the xylem of the late bloomers? Most have wood that displays large numbers of vessels, structures shaped like drinking straws that carry water to the leaves. Unlike the wood of maples and basswood, those vessels are concentrated in the early growth of the annual ring, the springwood. This condition is called "ring porous," and is associated with trees that leaf out late in spring. Ring porous trees produce wide-diameter vessels after threat of frost, and for a good reason. Ice in vessels can end up forming air bubbles as it melts. Bubbles in the vascular system of a plant are like blood clots traveling in our arteries. They can result in severe injury and death.

So it is that certain trees need more time to leaf out in spring. In the end, since they are competing very well with their upstart rivals, they must have other features that make up for their late start. Oaks are doing quite well in habitats that favor them.

Before we leave this topic of water transport in plants, I must

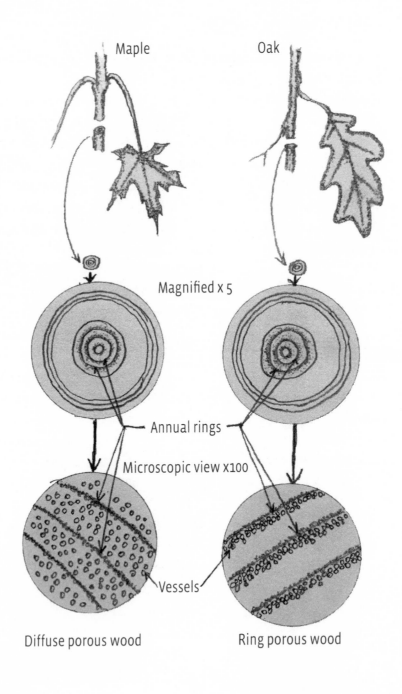

Maple

Oak

Magnified x 5

Annual rings

Microscopic view x100

Vessels

Diffuse porous wood

Ring porous wood

lay out a problem that has always puzzled me: How does sap rise in trees in spring? What drives it up the trunk and into the branches and twigs? Biology books are clear about how it goes up when leaves are present. The sun evaporates water from the leaves and pulls up the water that fills xylem cells from the roots to the leaves at the top of the tree. Of course, those dreaded bubbles must be avoided at all cost because that would short circuit the whole process. But how does a maple tree pump all that sugar-laden sap up the tree in March if there are no leaves? Usually, the water ascending the tree is just water with no sugar at all—sugar is carried down the stem by another tissue, the phloem. But, for a brief few weeks, that rule is violated as the xylem carries food to developing leaf buds. Does that have something to do with the force that propels sap up the tree? I don't know, but at those moments I lie tossing and turning without sleep, the question engages me. Most likely a clever scientist will figure it out soon, if she hasn't already. In a way, that might satisfy my curiosity, another crevice filled with knowledge, but sometimes it is nice to experience the fertile emptiness of a question unanswered. I shouldn't worry, though. Those questions pop up like mushrooms after a summer rain, even as the older questions disappear.

Transient hills and valleys of water waves

The wind had been blowing fiercely for eight hours, but a sharp shift in direction from southeast to due west occurred an hour or two ago. As I looked out on the waters of Boardman Lake, I could see waves coming in from the southwest, perhaps about thirty centimeters high, lapping on the sandy shore, one every three seconds or so. Looking more carefully, I saw another wave pattern, smaller waves of shorter period superimposed on the larger ones, these coming from the west—surely the result of the recent wind shift. Studying the waves for another minute, I could see another action: when the larger ones reached the shore, they broke and rebounded. Three activities happening all at once: the older, larger waves, the smaller ones from the west, and the rebounds. It all describes what sailors call a "chop," a somewhat haphazard play of wind on water that makes for a poorly defined pattern of wave action.

A chop close to shore does not mean that there is a short distance between crest and trough. At times waves reinforce each other, the crest towering high for a moment, while at others the troughs coincide, making a deeper valley in the water. Then there are the times when crest and trough came together, canceling each other out, erasing the wave altogether. The interplay of the three waves entranced me: I stood and watched them until I forgot about time. Afterwards, I resolved to learn as much as I could about water waves.

Assuming a lake is not shallow, three factors influence the size of waves: wind speed, duration of wind blowing in a given direction, and fetch (the distance wind travels over open water). Online, Planetcalc (https://planetcalc.com/4442/) offers a means of calculating the size of a wave, and I had to try it out. Entering a wind speed 32 km/hr (20 mph), a duration of six hours of wind from the southeast, and a fetch of 3.2 km (2 miles), the answer came out to be .4 meters (1 ft 4 in), a reasonable estimate for Boardman Lake. Playing with the calculator, a wind speed of 50 mph blowing for six hours gives a wave height of about three meters (about 10 feet). Such waves occur on the Great Lakes, especially in the late autumn. In 1975, the freighter Edmund Fitzgerald went down in such a sea with all lives lost.

Large waves attract interest from us all. In my town, when the wind blows hard out of the northwest, people often visit the waterfront to watch the waves crash into the shore. Water is flying about everywhere, and it takes resolution to get out of the car and get close to the action. The rebound of waves off the metal barrier creates stupendous mountains of water, building and subsiding in a hypnotic manner. Out from shore, whitecaps are everywhere, waves breaking far from land. Scientists have determined that when the wind speed is 1.3 times the speed of the wave, whitecaps begin to appear. Of course, waves break when they reach shallow water even when that rule is not in effect.

Let us look at the other end the scale: ripples. Technically, they can be defined as waves that have a period (the time elapsed between the arrival of two crests) of three seconds or less. The wind speed for such wavelets is between three and eleven km/hr (2-7 mph). The calculator gives their height as 10 cm or about 4 inches. It seems to me that the distinction between ripples and waves is arbitrary, though, for all that, I am glad the English language separates the terms. A ripple is a friendly thing, suggesting mild winds and ruffled water, while a wave can be something mighty and destructive. While big waves can sink ships, ripples have gentler effects. They can illuminate a watery pathway to the rising or setting sun or moon, a *glitter path*. If the water was absolutely still, only the round reflection of sun or moon would reach our eyes, with no pathway visible at all. While that phenomenon can overwhelm us, so does the roadway that leads us out over the water to the orbs themselves.

Before leaving this topic, I would mention my favorite kind of ripple, the ripples formed when raindrops strike the water's surface. They appear everywhere as rain begins to fall, eventually disappearing in a chop as the rain picks up. The first ones cover a glassy expanse of water with concentric circles that expand and disappear, each bringing joy to the human heart. Their transience reflects the transience of all living things, lingering for a moment only to pass away as others take their place. The Buddhist poet Issa, remembering the passing of one of his children, writes this haiku:

> *the world of dew*
> *is a world of dew*
> *and yet, and yet...*

He could have been talking about the falling of raindrops on a still pond.

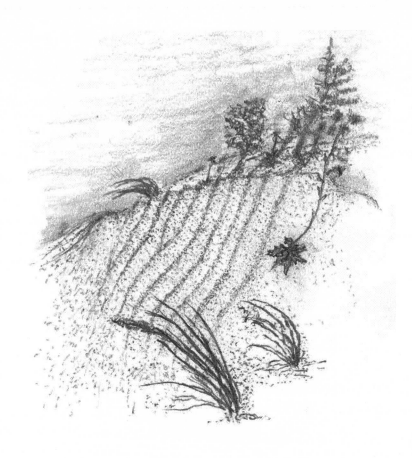

Ripples give form to wind and water

It is not always necessary to search for interesting things: they are in plain sight all along. So it was one day when I was searching the foredune along a Great Lakes beach for rare plants. Among patches of wormwood, poison ivy, and rock cress, in exposed areas avoided by foot traffic of beachgoers, I noticed ripples in the sand, the crests perhaps five centimeters apart (2 in), the depth not much over a centimeter. An unbroken array of them appeared in the rise and fall of miniature swales and hills, the distance covered by the disturbed sand one to several meters long. Surely, they were not rare phenomena, since, no doubt, I had walked over them unthinkingly for many years, though only now, for the first time, I paid attention to them, and began to ask questions. How are they formed? With respect to the wind, how are they oriented? Do they move as water ripples do? How fast does the wind have to blow in order to start ripple formation? As Sherlock Holmes was fond of saying, "Come, Watson, come. The game is afoot." A new investigation opened itself to me.

The day before my outing to the beach, for most of the daylight hours, the wind had blown steadily from the southwest at a velocity of 15 miles per hour (24 km) with gusts certainly higher. With no trees to block it, the foredune would have been the perfect place to make waves in the sand, especially since most visiting humans and their pets stayed close to the water, as their footprints amply demonstrated. Not carrying a compass, but having a rudimentary sense of direction, I observed the ripples were oriented parallel to an east-west line. Were they perpendicular to yesterday's wind? It seemed so.

Though direct observation is preferable to second-hand research, I explored layman's literature for anything I could find about sand ripples. *Scientific American* did not disappoint: a short article published in October, 1999, authored by Robert S. Anderson and Walt Hoagman of Michigan State University, offered insight into the formation of sand ripples. Sure enough, they were formed in a direction perpendicular to the direction of the wind. Their wavelength—the distance from crest to crest—depended on the velocity of the wind,

Sand Ripple Cross-section

the longer wavelengths associated with higher winds. If the wind had been blowing at thirty miles per hour (50 kmh), fast enough to make me feel the sting of windblown sand grains on my ankles, the ripples would have been more widely spaced.

Sand ripples are not symmetrical on cross-section. They have a gentle slope (stoss) from which the wind picks up sand grains, and a steep one (lee) where they are deposited. As the wind speed increases, the "wind shadow" of the lee side (the area of diminished wind) lengthens, making the wave crests farther apart. Sand grains dance in the flow, rising up in the air and descending, the impact launching another grain to fly up only to crash into another. At low wind speeds their flight might only cover a few millimeters, but as speeds increase, it can lengthen to many centimeters. Only then can you feel the prickle on your ankles as you walk through the sand. The name of the dance is saltation, a word that stems from Latin, the root word meaning "to jump." If it is a dance, it is a violent one, more akin to bumper cars than square dances.

Walt Hoagman asserts that wind ripples are rare on Great Lakes shores, and in one sense, he is surely right. It is hard to find massive sand ripples on beaches because of disturbance by humans and by the fickle nature of winds in the area, constantly changing direction and dying down after only a few hours of action. If the sand on western dunes forms whitecaps, then the sand of Michigan forms only the smallest waves. With regard to the movement of ripples, Hoagman comments that the period of the ripples—the time it takes for successive crests to pass a point—is on the order of days. On our beaches, it is hard to imagine a wind blowing from the same direction for that long.

Before leaving the topic of land ripples, let us consider the phenomenon of washboarding, the process that results in ripples in the substrate of gravel roads as a result of vehicle traffic. Unlike sand ripples, it depends on human intervention for its existence. The more drastic the action imposed on roads, the greater the effects: For example, more vehicles and faster speeds cause bigger bumps. According to a study conducted at Cambridge University in 2007, almost all substrates produce the ripples: fine sand through coarse gravel, wet or dry. Speed is critical; the threshold speed for development is about five miles per hour (8 kmh). Modern suspension systems designed to provide a smooth ride do not affect washboard roads since wheels without any suspension system create the bumps just as well. A friend of mine imagined that, if you went fast enough, the jarring would diminish as the wheels travelled from crest to crest. Aside from the danger of going that fast on a rural road, that behavior would make washboarding worse for other drivers. In the end, it might be better to go less than five miles per hour—providing you have the patience and the time.

OUT OF THE CORNER OF YOUR EYE

Besides wind, sand ripples can occur because of flowing water in a stream or small waves in the shallows of a sandy beach. On the same day I noticed sand ripples caused by the wind, I saw them in the shallows of Boardman Lake. Stirred up by the wind above, they, too, were oriented perpendicular to the wind. When I searched for them a day later, they were gone. Presumably contrary wave action had erased them.

Waves and ripples are all around us, on water, on land, and—invisibly—in the air in the form of sound waves (though those are of a different nature). In one of its aspects, light is a wave, too, expressing itself by means of reflection, refraction, and dispersion, all wave characteristics. Waves are a basic expression of Nature's patterns, perhaps the fundamental one. Let us become more aware of them as we go about our lives, visiting lakes, sunning ourselves on a beach, or experiencing a bouncing ride on a gravel road. In the ebb and flow of things, are not we waves, too?

Ripples give form to wind and water

Here is my take on wind and waves:

> *touch, fingers of wind,*
> *touch the sand and touch*
> *shape the ripples and touch*
> *finger them along, and touch*
> *then leave them in repose.*
>
> *touch, fingers of wind,*
> *touch the water, and touch*
> *build the waves and touch*
> *palm them along, and touch*
> *then leave them be to rest*
>
> *touch, fingers of wind,*
> *touch my skin, and touch*
> *grow my being, and touch*
> *nudge it along, and touch*
> *then leave it kissed and blessed*

The watchstone

Fossils have always fascinated me. Having grown up in a state littered with stones brought by the glaciers (Michigan), there are plenty of them lying around, the most common showing traces of corals, bryozoans (moss animals), and the shells of many organisms. Donut-shaped crinoids were easy finds, the shape of the donuts not hinting at the stalked forms that waved about gracefully in the warm currents of a Devonian ocean. I was saddened that dinosaur fossils were unlikely to be found near my childhood home but a kind-hearted fifth grade teacher eased the pain by gifting me with a chip from a Tyrannosaurus fossil bone.

The watchstone

In my imagination, I could see the animal that harbored it, blood-thirsty and ready for confrontations with Triceratops or other such creatures.

Now I wonder if I hadn't dismissed those simpler fossils of warm seas too quickly. Though less violent than reptile carnivores, no doubt corals and bryozoans had stories to tell, and a skillful writer could paint a nuanced and colorful picture of their lives, but that is not the story I wish to tell here. Instead, I want to tell how a fossil could affect the life of one person, a child separated from the familiarities of our world by a wide gulf in time and culture.

A fossil coral, called a Petoskey stone by locals, is found along beaches near my home and is widely sold in rock shops and jewelry stores along the shores of Northern Michigan. Polished, they are magnificent as displayed in rings, necklaces, or pendants; unpolished, they still attract interest—especially to rock hunters. Hundreds of people look for them at beaches, some of them wading in freezing water to harvest them with a cup attached to a pole so that they do not have to get soaked going after the deep ones. As a consequence every beach house has a dozen or more on its grounds. No doubt, a future archaeologist will wonder at the phenomenon of the disproportion of Petoskey stones associated with those residences. Surely, it will be ascribed to a cultural value peculiar to that society.

What follows is a story of an interaction between a Petoskey stone and a human being that came to treasure it. It is fiction, but, at same time, it could be true—the face all good fiction presents. At the outset, I wish to make it clear that nothing in the following story is taken from Odawa or Ojibwe legend. I would not plunder that treasure trove of wisdom.

The watchstone

The howling drew nearer, as the wolves were emboldened by hunger. They rarely intruded upon the camps of men, but now, in the deepest and coldest days of winter, they ventured close, perhaps to take a dog barking at their darting shadows or to steal from the food stores guarded by Wahtohe. Scant snow blew from the branches of cedars, giving form to the wind. The haloed moon glowed overhead, full and high in the sky, though muted in its light as if seen through milky ice.

Shoshoe could not sleep, but it was not because of the cold. A pile of deerskins was heaped upon her, their weight and scent a familiar marker of the season. Layered three deep and densely covered with the fur that had warmed the animals only a few months before, they provided ample protection from the cold. Besides, the embers of the fire were still red within the firepit at one end of the long house, the dying fire taking the edge off the chill. And the birch bark that formed the skin of the shelter did not let in the wind; her father, Oshii, had made sure of that, caulking the joints with moss and balsam pitch before the ice had formed on the lake.

Ordinarily she would sleep the night through, within the tiny cave formed and heated by her body, but this night was different. It was not merely the sounds of the wolf or the distant call of an owl that made her sit up suddenly, but something that made almost no sound at all. She had heard the elders tell the stories late at night of the Kin'shain, the dark being that stole light and life from the villages of men. It lived within the shadows and was never seen when looked at, only appearing unexpectedly at the edge of vision, darting away like a fleeing bat. This was what lurked nearby, the Kin'shain that dwelled beyond her sight, waiting to do harm to her and the ones she loved.

She called out to her mother who shared her sleeping space. "Shoge, wake up! There is something out there!"

Pushing at her mother's broad back, she felt her breathing change and heard a quiet moan from the other side of the sleeping place. "Sleep, daughter, sleep," came the words of her mother, foggy with dreams. "The dawn is long to come."

But Shoshoe could not rest, and she laid a trembling hand against her mother's back again. "There is something out there, something black and I am afraid."

"It is but the things of the night, the wolf and the owl. Sleep, Precious One, and the light of the day will brighten your spirit."

They were silent for a moment, and then Shoge's breathing

took on the rhythm of sleep. Shoshoe burrowed deeply under the deerskins.

But Kin'shain had not gone away. Shoshoe could feel his presence, and he was drawing near. She could stay still no longer and bounded away from the sleeping place, the mats spread upon the ground surprising her feet with the cold. In a single motion she grasped a deerskin robe and wrapped it about her shoulders. At the same time, she jumped into her beaded moccasins, arranged side-by-side by the sleeping platform. Without sound, she approached the firepit, took out a torch stick from the bundle kept by the fire, and thrust it into the embers. It sputtered and burst into flame, the balsam pitch at the tip flaring brightly as it ignited the cattail fuel below. The flickering light illuminated the inside of the long house dimly at first, but with growing brilliance. Shoshoe did not wish to wake her mother, and she quickly ducked her head low to push through the entrance of her bark home, taking care to keep the torch's flame away from the birch bark skin that held back the winter's cold.

Outside, the cold stung her cheeks and her breath formed white clouds that streamed from her nose. A few snow-flakes were carried by the wind, landing upon her robe, her hair, and her face, lingering a moment before melting. As she held up the torch, the flame danced and the shadows of nearby things flickered and played on the snow.

The watchstone

She was grateful for its light, for she knew that darkness was a friend to Kin'shain. The flame would chase him away, at least for this night.

Silently she walked, listening for the tiny sounds that spoke his presence, watching for the darting shadow that gives him away. The long house was a dark shadow behind her now, yet she kept walking, the night's cold gradually overcoming the warmth of sleep. Only a few more steps, a few more to chase Kin'shain away from this place: it would not be long.

Then she heard the sounds: a low growl and the tearing of flesh. She peered at the grove of cedar ahead and tried to make sense of the dark shapes she saw shadowed against the snow. As she watched, a single dark form bent low over another, and it was eating it—she was sure of it—the white gleam of its teeth left no doubt. With a low growl it suddenly looked up and stared at her. Kin'shain had sensed her presence, and she held the torch high to proclaim its brightness. But her movement was too rapid. The wind had extinguished its flame.

Shoshoe turned and ran for the long house outlined against the snow in the distance. She heard the gallop of Kin'shain behind her, the sounds of its steps muffled against the snow, and heard its rasping breath.

"Aiiya!" she called out, "It comes to eat me! Help me, mother, help me!" Without looking back, she ducked into the low door of the long house and found herself in the warmth and silence of her home. Stripping off her wet robe and kicking off her moccasins, she tumbled into the pile of deerskins where her mother lay. She stirred—she had heard her daughter's wild cry as she approached—and turned to stare at her young daughter who pressed so close to her.

"What is it, Precious One? Why do you tremble and shake?"

"Kin'shain!" she could only say. "He comes! He chased me here and now he comes to eat me!"

Shoge stroked her daughter's hair and spoke quietly. "It is only a dream. Now, rest and all will be well."

"But I saw him outside. He was eating another. He saw me and came running." She burrowed deep into the deerskins and shuddered with fear.

Shoge rose and listened to the wind whip the branches of the cedars. The night was quiet. Even the wolves had stopped their calls. She slipped into her moccasins and pulled on her robe. Walking past the empty sleeping places of Oshii and her son Oreho, she felt a pang of sorrow for their absence. Soon they would return from their journey to visit Grandma on the shore of the Great Water, yet on nights like this she missed them especially. Shoshoe would sleep better with her father and brother at home. She was so young—only six summers had passed since her birth—and she woke up afraid on many nights like this. At such times the low voice of her father would still her fear and she would return to sleep. Tonight, Shoge would have to calm her daughter.

Bending low to leave the long house, Shoge heard her daughter's plea. "Do not go out, Mother. He waits for us!"

"I only go out to see what is there. I will not leave you, Shoshoe." Shoge stepped out into the night's cold.

Outside, the sky showed a few stars through the thin clouds driven by the wind. The full moon was bright upon the snow, and shadows were black upon its surface. The running footprints of Shoshoe made a pathway that extended to the cedars beyond. Nothing stirred, save a wisp of snow swept from a snowdrift nearby. Her eyes to the ground, Shoge pursued her daughters' footprints in a slow lope. What had scared her so?

Approaching the cedar grove, other prints could be seen, and blood upon the snow. It was the track of Washoe, the wolf, and it had made its kill here. Tufts of fur were scattered about and a piece of bone with flesh still attached stuck out from the red-stained snow. Washoe! It was Washoe that had frightened her daughter so, not Kin'shain, as she had told.

When Shoge reentered the long house, Shoshoe called out, "Mother, is it you? Was Kin'shain out there? Does he wait for us?"

"No, Precious One. He was not there. It was Washoe, the wolf, who frightened you. He made his kill near the cedar grove. It was only Washoe. You may rest easily now and go to sleep."

"Washoe? No, it was Kin'shain. He was black with white teeth and he stole the light from the moon. He chased me and tried to take the light of my soul. He will come back, Mother."

"It is time for sleep, little one." And she began the song of sleep she had learned from her own mother:

> *The day is done, lay down your care.*
> *The day is done, lay down your sorrow.*
> *The day is done, a new day will come.*
> *Now sleep, precious one, sleep.*

The watchstone

She sang for a long time, until she felt her young daughter enter the land of sleep.

It was spring. The trailing arbutus opened its small flowers within sight of grainy wet snowbanks. The sound of water was everywhere, dripping from branches and gurgling in creeks. The call of the red-winged blackbird sounded across the marsh and at night, the first spring peepers spoke loudly to each other.

Spring came to the world of men, too. The winter shelters were taken down, the precious birch bark carefully rolled up to be carried to the summer village. Winter robes were packed away in boxes of cedar lashed together with strips of black ash, and the fires burned bright at night as the village came together for drums and song and tales of the elders. Voices were raised by the children in play later now, as the days grew longer. They were as joyful as the birds newly returned from the south.

During the daytime, Shoshoe felt the joy, too. But at night, the spirit of Kin'shain lurked about her sleeping place. She could not forget the black shape, the white fangs, the growl, and the snap of a bone. It was not Washoe, the wolf, but Kin'shain disguised as a wolf. He awaited her and would find her if she let down her guard. That was why she did not sleep at night and why Shoge would sing to quiet her restlessness. It took much singing before the little girl could go to sleep—even with Oshii and Oreho nearby. In her own sleeplessness, her mother worried for her little one.

One day, as mother and daughter walked upon the beach of the Great Water, they came upon something wonderful. At their feet was a stone about the size of Shoshoe's hand. It was brown like the earth, with rays shooting out from many places upon its surface. It shone in the wetness and looked out with many eyes. They turned it over and over and saw that eyes covered it on all sides.

"It looks everywhere," the young girl said with awe in her voice.

"Its eyes are always open. It never sleeps," said Shoge.

"It fades as it dries. I wish to make it shine. When it shines, the eyes watch out for me."

"Your father knows how to make stones shine. Let us bring it to him. He will polish it and then it will be yours."

So it was that Oshii made the watchstone bright and smooth. He gave it to his daughter, Shoshoe, in a small deerskin pouch which she came to carry on a cord around her neck. At night she took it out of its pouch and placed it beside her sleeping place to guard against Kin'shain. She knew it would wake her if danger came. She slept easy now.

Shoshoe had many sons and daughters and lived to a great old age. Her face was wrinkled like the bark of the elm and her hair was white as the herring gull's feathers. Always she carried her watchstone around her neck: throughout the births of her children, throughout their sicknesses and in their good health, throughout their marriages and the births of her grandchildren, throughout the years of plenty and the years of want. When times were hard, she would take the stone out and hold it in her hand, feeling its soothing coolness. And she would remember its power to conquer fear—the fear she had felt so long ago as a little girl.

When Shoshoe died, the watchstone was buried with her. It watched over her then, too, as she entered the spirit world and her bones returned to the earth. It watches over her even now.

Richard Fidler taught seventh and ninth grade science for thirty-one years in Traverse City, Michigan. He loves ferns, flowering plants, jumping spiders, ant lions, map turtles, and belted kingfishers. The University of Michigan Biological Station provided a foundation for those interests, and he is forever indebted to the professors there who helped him to wake up to the natural world. His academic leanings drove him to earn a B.A. in East Asian Languages, a B.A. in Biology, an M.S. in Biology, and later an Ed. D. in Science Education, all from the U of M. After finishing his career in education, he became an author, writing seven books about history and nature. Presently, he lives along the Boardman River in Traverse City, enjoying the ripples of rain on the water, the shadows of overhanging boxelder trees, and occasional visits of a Great Blue Heron. Besides those delights, he participates in get-togethers with his wife, two children, and four grandchildren. How lucky he is!

Other books by Richard Fidler

In some places history lurks just under the surface. An old factory whispers a story about its workers a hundred years ago. An ancient oak with its trunk curiously bent suggests times before white settlement. GATEWAYS TO GRAND TRAVERSE PAST identifies these magical places and tells the stories connected with them. Illustrated.

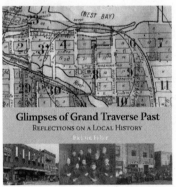

In discussions focused on important historical events, artifacts, and institutions of the Grand Traverse area, GLIMPSES OF GRAND TRAVERSE PAST explores who we are and how we got that way. Illustrated with archived photographs, it presents a refreshingly new perspective on Grand Traverse history.

Not so long ago, we spent our hours enjoying life in a world of hunting and fishing, playing card games and working jigsaw puzzles, reading books and writing postcards, making music and listening to it. We sat and talked with our friends, we celebrated our holidays modestly, but well. Sometimes, we smoked and we drank.

HOW THE GOOD TIMES ROLLED tells how we used to take joy in life before the digital age. It reminds us that the real world of nature—and of flesh-and-blood people—offers the greatest reward of happiness. Illustrated.

One hundred-sixty-five years ago the Boardman River emptied its waters into the West Arm of Grand Traverse Bay amid a vast forest of white pines, red pines, and oak trees. But for occasional villages of Odawa Indians, the area was largely uninhabited. Sixty years later, the forests had disappeared, replaced by factories, an asylum, schools, and churches as a primitive settlement grew into a small town. In time, the community shrank as residents moved away in search of better lives. Still, change was not done: people began to return, seeking the grace the land and water offered them as they reinvented the basis upon which their lives were built. This is the story of Traverse City, Michigan and it is the story of this book.

Illustrated with historic photographs and aerial views of Traverse City.

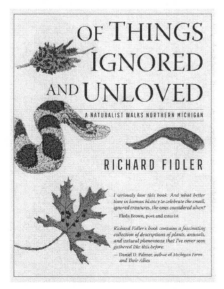

We respect wolves, hawks and bobcats, love songbirds and lilies, and are moved by a sunset observed through pine boughs, but we do not care for poison ivy or winged ants. We ignore lichens even though we see them growing on trees everywhere, and we may not even know the names of other things that occupy our world: ventifacts, grape ferns, and club mosses. This book will awaken the reader to events and things tuned out and forgotten in the noisy, rushing environment of our lives. It is a safari to nearby places.

Illustrated by the author.

Books available locally or at Amazon.

Made in the USA
Middletown, DE
21 October 2021